Lights for Luucy
by Connie Dunn

A Unitarian Universalist Celebration of Winter Holidays

Lights for Luucy: A Unitarian Universalist Celebration of Winter Holidays © 2013 Connie Dunn

Published by Nature Woman Wisdom Press

First Edition. Printed and bound in the United States of America.

All rights reserved. No part of this book may be reproduced in any form or by any electronic or mechanical means, including information storage and retrieval systems, recording, or photocopying, without permission in writing from the publisher, except by a reviewer, who may quote brief passages in review or where permitted by law.

Copyright © 2013 Connie Dunn
ISBN-13: 978-0615888484
ISBN-10: 0615888488

Published by Nature Woman Wisdom Press
Printed in The United States of America
September, 2013
9 8 7 6 5 4 3 2

Library of Congress Cataloging in Publication Data

Dunn, Connie
Lights for Luucy: A Unitarian Universalist Celebration of Winter Holidays

Celebration
    Lights for Luucy: A Unitarian Universalist Celebration of Winter Holidays
    by Connie Dunn
Unitarian Universalist
    Lights for Luucy: A Unitarian Universalist Celebration of Winter Holidays
    by Connie Dunn
Winter Celebration Stories
    Lights for Luucy: A Unitarian Universalist Celebration of Winter Holidays
    by Connie Dunn

For my daughters, Michelle and Erin with special thanks to Michelle for her editing.

For my granddaughter, Destiny.

For Sophia Rose and her continued support and wonderful Flaming Chalice Cookie Cutters!

For ALL Unitarian Universalists, especially Families who look for inclusive celebrations for their children.

For All People of Faith and for All the Celebrations of Faith in Our Wonderful World.

Illustrations were done in felt by Connie Dunn, then photographed. Some pictures were offered by ChalicePalice.com. Other pictures used were composites of many photos or stock photos.

Luucy or LUUcy is not a typo, it is intentional to emphasize UU (Unitarian Universalism).

The symbol of our Unitarian Universalist faith is a flame within a chalice (a cup with a stem and foot, similar to a goblet or champagne glass and the chalice for which many Christian faiths use as a symbol of the Wine that Jesus shared at the Last Supper).

"At the opening of Unitarian Universalist worship services, many congregations light a flame inside a chalice. This flaming chalice has become a well-known symbol of our denomination. It unites our members in worship and symbolizes the spirit of our work." —Dan Hotchkiss SOURCE: Unitarian Universalist Association (www.uua.org)

Hans Deutsch, an Austrian artist, first brought together the chalice and the flame as a Unitarian symbol during his work with the Unitarian Service Committee during World War II. To Deutsch, the image had connotations of sacrifice and love. Unitarian Universalists today have many different interpretations of the image. To learn more about the history of our Unitarian Universalist symbol, please go to http://www.uua.org/beliefs/chalice/151248.shtml

Lights for Luucy

When Luucy was just nine years old, she began to wonder about all the winter holidays and how they could come together in one big celebration.

"Hi! I'm Luucy. Come with me to learn about my special celebration of winter holidays and how everyone celebrates in their own way!"

"One of my friends, Ambar, comes from India where they celebrate *Divali*, which is the Hindu harvest festival," says Luucy.

"It is called *The Festival of Lights*, which I thought I'd call my special Unitarian Universalist Celebration. Come with me to see how each of these fall and winter celebrations are about light!"

In India, *Diwali* or *Divali* (Dee-vahl-lee) is celebrated by honoring Laksmi, (Lahx-smee) the goddess of good fortunes. This celebration is also called *the Festival of Lights.*, brv

Luucy liked the idea of lighting lots of candles. And she loved fireworks, too!

Source:
This is a compilation of many familiar images that you might see during the Hindu Celebration of Divali or the Hindu Festival of Lights and Laksmi, the Hindu Goddess of Good Fortune.

In India, the houses have beautiful drawings made with powdered rice, limestone, or chalk. These drawings are called *Ringoli Designs* and grace the doorways of the homes in India. These designs are also known as *Mandalas*, which are Sanskrit spiritual symbols. Hindu and Buddhist Monks often create these as a spiritual meditation.

Source:
Society for the Confluence of Festivals in India

Divali is a five-day celebration, which falls somewhere between the middle of October and the middle of November. It's a family celebration. One of the names for *Diwali* is

Deepavali, which translates to: *a row of lamps.* Just as colorful as the *Ringolis* are the paper lanterns. The streets are lit with all sorts of lamps from simple clay lamps to sophisticated street lamps. Inside the houses, small lamps are also lit. And the paper lanterns are everywhere.

Source: Dreamstime.com

Another tradition is getting up before dawn on the third day of the festival and taking a bath while the stars are still shining and then dressing in new clothes.

This festival is just as much cultural as it is religious; the Hindus, Sikhs, and Jains celebrate *Divali.* It is also popular in America, especially with school children.

Luucy loved lights and candles. Her family always lit a candle in their chalice at mealtime.

They each said something they were grateful for. Luucy loved family dinners almost as much as learning about the fall and winter celebrations of her friends.

"Come meet, Ilana! She's my Jewish friend. In the winter, the Jewish people celebrate Hanukkah," says Luucy.

Hanukkah is a Jewish celebration that honors a miracle that happened in about 175 B.C.E. (Today's years are referred to as AD or CE, which simply means the *Current Era* or "Anno Domini," the Latin translation of "the year of our Lord. B.C.E. stands for *Before the Current Era*). In 175 B.C.E., there was a war, and the Syrian-Greeks took over the Jewish Temples.

Source: Archives Photo of an Ancient Temple

The Maccabees led a war of independence and defeated the Syrian-Greek army. When they returned to the Temple and lit the *Lamp of Life*, there was only a tiny amount of oil.

But this flame lasted for eight days, long enough for messengers to return with a full store of oil. Today, the Menorah has eight candles to represent this miracle.

Another tradition is to play the Dreidel game, which is usually played for gold-coin-wrapped chocolate! Luucy liked chocolate, so she liked this game!

"Hi, again," Luucy says. "I want to introduce, Diana. Her family is Pagan and they celebrate the Winter Solstice, which is the longest night of the year. Diana and I are having fun feeding the birds."

Diana's family were all about being friendly to the earth and all its creatures. Luucy told her friend that honoring the earth was one of her Unitarian Universalist Principles. Luucy and Diana happily fed the birds!

The celebration is in honor of the returning light. Diana decorates a Solstice Tree and attends a celebration with lots of dancing around a bonfire.

Some cultures burn a "Yule" log as part of the celebration. Winter Solstice is an ancient celebration, which was a weeklong festival in Roman times. Each year, they feasted and honored the God Saturn, which focuses on the rebirth of the Sun God, which honors the renewal or lengthening of daylight.

"Come with me!" says Luucy. "I want you to meet Marta, her family comes from Sweeden. They celebrate Santa Lucia (pronounced San-ta Lu-Chee-Ah), which translates to Saint Lucy in English! I think I'm going to like this celebration...wonder how you become a Saint?"

Luucy went to the library and learned more about this tradition.

She and Marta decorated wreaths, which the girls wear on their heads with candles lit and deliver sweet breakfast bread to their parents.

In Sweden and other countries in the northern parts of Europe, she learned that the oldest girl in the family would get up early on Santa Lucia Day and bake the traditional breakfast breads and don a crown of evergreen and candles as she served her parents and the rest of the family breakfast.

Marta did that in her house!

In more recent years, the tradition has included boys as Star Boys.

Marta's brother, Otto, helped bring the sweet bread to their parents on December 13.

Luucy says, "Come with me, again. I want you to meet Anna. Her family is Christian!"

Christian families celebrate Christmas, the birth of Christ or Jesus. They hang lights on a Christmas tree, sometimes inside and out! They even put them around the roof of their house and put many other decorations in the yard, like Jesus in a manger (a feeding container, usually found in a barn) with Joseph and Mary.

With Anna, Luucy sang Christmas Hymns and decorated a tree!

Luucy went to Shawna's house to learn about Kwanza.

"Hi!" says Luucy. "Shawna is African-American, and on December 26, her family celebrates *Kwanzaa* for seven days! They light a candle for each day."

The candles are on a *Kinara.*, which is somewhat like a candelabra! Each day they light another candle.

Kwanza is the only truly American-made light celebration. It honors the gathering together of family, the commemoration of ancestors, the re-dedication to growth of the community and the offering of gratitude for life's good. To get this celebration started, money was required to spread the word. It was partially funded by the Unitarian Universalist Association.

Kwanzaa is also a harvest celebration!

As a Unitarian Universalist (UU), Luucy learned about many traditions. And though they were all very wonderful celebrations, they all belonged to other religions or cultures. Luucy wondered what sort of celebration she should have as a UU? And so, with help from her family, Luucy created one.

Luucy loved the *Festival of Lights* as the name of her celebration, even though she was borrowing it from India's *Divali* and the Jewish *Hannukah* celebrations.

So when other children were celebrating the harvests with *Divali* and *Halloween*, Luucy was baking Chalice cookies.

Luucy's mother helped her freeze them to keep them fresh until they could distribute them.

At Thanksgiving when others were baking pies and roasting turkeys, Luucy was baking Chalice cookies.

Although her family did carve pumpkins for Halloween and bake a turkey for Thanksgiving.

When everyone else was baking *Christmas* and *Hanukkah* cookies, Luucy baked Chalice cookies in all varieties includes those with M&Ms and chocolate chunks. And when her friends were celebrating *Kwanzaa*, Luucy was still baking Chalice cookies.

When most of her friends were playing with the toys they had received for the various holidays, Luucy began her own special *UU Festival of Lights* celebration.

She lit all the candles for *Divali* and said the Laksmi chant:

Aum Sring Hring Kleeng Maha Lakxmaye Namah Aum

She lit the candles on the Menorah for *Hanukkah* and said the *Hanukkah* blessing:

*Ba-rooch a-ta a-do-nai, el-o-hey-nu
me-lech ha-o-lam
a-sher kid-shah-nu b'mitz-vo-tav,
v'tzee-va-nu l'*
had-leek ner, shel Ha-nuk-kah

*Blessed are You, Lord our God, King of
the Universe,
who has sanctified us with His
commandments and
commanded us to kindle the Hanukkah
lights.*

She lit candles for the *Solstice* and said the blessing:

Blessings on this day, the Winter Solstice.
Blessings for the sun that it might return once more.
Blessings for the people that light might shine in their hearts.
Blessings for the earth that life grows deep in its womb.
Blessings on the people that peace might prevail.
Blessings on this Winter Solstice day.
Blessed be!

She lit more candles for *Santa Lucia* and recited the words of the wake-up song:

Through snowy winter days
Thy song comes winging.
To waken earth again
Glad Carols bringing.
Come thou, O Queen of Light
Wearing thy crown so bright.
Santa Lucia! Santa Lucia!

Brightly the silver star
Shines o'er the ocean.
Fair winds woo billows
Calmly in motion,
My bark shall fleetly glide
Over the sea, ah!
Santa Lucia! Santa Lucia!

Luucy lit the candles for *Christmas* and said a *Christmas* prayer:

When the song of angels is stilled,
When the star in the sky is gone,
When the kings and princes are home,
When the shepherds are back with their flock,
The work of Christmas begins:
to find the lost,
to heal the broken,
to feed the hungry,
to release the prisoner,
to rebuild the nations,
to bring peace among the brothers,
to make music in the heart.

Luucy lit the *Kwanzaa* Kinara candles.

She recited the prayers for each day:

Habari gani?(hah-bar-ee gah-nee)
We light the first Kwanzaa candle,
the black candle, to celebrate umoja,
unity.

Habara gani? We light the second
Kwanzaa candle,
a red candle to represent
kujichagulia (koo-jee-cha-goo-lee-ah),
self-determination or learning the
traditions that help us define
ourselves.

Source: USPS Stamp
http://www.shape.org/Kwanzaa.asp

*Habari gani? We light the third Kwanzaa candle,
a green candle to honor
ujima (oo-jee-mah), responsibility.*

*Habari gani? We light the fourth Kwanzaa candle,
a red candle to celebrate ujama (oo-jah-maah),
cooperative economics.*

*Source: USPS Stamp
http://www.shape.org/Kwanzaa.asp*

*Habari gani? We light the fifth Kwanzaa candle,
a green candle to reflect nia (nee-ah),
illuminate our purpose.*

*Habari gani? We light the sixth
Kwanzaa candle,
a red candle to celebrate
kuumba (ku-oom-bah),
creativity.*

Source: Dreamstime.com

*Habari gani? We light the seventh
Kwanzaa candle
to honor imani (ee-mahn-ee), faith.*

Then, Luucy lit her most sacred of all the lights. She lit the *Chalice* and recited all seven Unitarian Universalist Principles:

We Believe:

1. *That each and every person is important;*

2. *That all people should be treated fairly and kindly;*

3. *That we should accept one another and keep on learning together;*

4. *That each person must be free to search for what is true and right in life;*

5. *That all persons should have a vote about the things that concern them;*

6. *In working for a peaceful, fair and free world; and*

7. *In caring for our planet earth, the home we share with all living things.*

Afterwards, Luucy delivered cookies to nursing homes, retirement homes and group homes for the mentally challenged. She delivered cookies to families that had been too poor to celebrate any holiday.

She delivered cookies to hospitals and police stations. She delivered cookies to friends and family. And with every package of cookies, Luucy had included a note.

It said:
> This is my *Unitarian Universalist Festival of Lights* celebration. The Chalice is a symbol of love that lights my life. And with these Chalice Cookies, I hope you find a spark of light from whatever Divine Entity you believe. As a Unitarian Universalist, we believe that each day like the first day of the year can be a new beginning of diversity, love, fairness and hope, because we are all part of the interdependent web of life.

*Holiday Card can be purchased at http://www.zazzle.com/sophiarosefineart

And when all the cookies had been delivered, Luucy said, "Mom, this was the best Holiday ever!"

Chalice Cookies

Make and bake cookies, then decorate with icing. See icing recipe below.

> 1 1/2 cups stick butter or margarine, softened
>
> 2 cups white granulated sugar
>
> 4 eggs
>
> 1 teaspoon vanilla extract
>
> 5 cups all-purpose flour
>
> 2 teaspoons baking powder
>
> 1 teaspoon salt

Directions

Preheat oven to 400 degrees Fahrenheit.

In a large bowl, cream (using the back of a large spoon press the together the butter and sugar) until smooth.

In a separate bowl, beat eggs with a whisk. Add the vanilla and the beaten eggs. Stir in the flour, baking powder, and salt. Mix well.

Cover the bowl, and chill in the dough in the refrigerator for at least one hour or overnight, when possible.

Roll out the dough with rolling pin on a floured surface to about 1/4 to 1/2 inch thickness.

Source:
http://www.chalicepalace.com

Using *Chalice Cookie Cutters (come in several sizes). Place the Chalice-shaped cookies on a baking sheet.

Bake 6 to 8 minutes in preheated oven. Cool completely.

*Chalice Cookie Cutters can be bought from http://www.chalicepalace.com/Chalice_Palace/Welcome.html

Chalice Cookie Icing

1 cup powdered sugar

1/2 teaspoon vanilla

1-2 tablespoons milk

Source:
http://www.chalicepalace.com/Chalice_Palace/Welcome.html

Directions

Mix powdered sugar, vanilla and milk, adding only 1 tablespoon of milk at a time.

The goal is to make the mixture thin enough to spread, but not so runny that it all runs off the cookie. Some people like to paint their cookies rather than to smear the icing onto the cookies. For painting, make the mixture thinner. If you get it too thin, add a tablespoon of powdered sugar at a time until it has gotten to the right consistency.

Source:
http://www.chalicepalace.com/

When icing sets, it makes a hard surface rather than a soft one, which means that the cookies are stackable and easy to handle without getting messy.

To decorate with colors, divide the mixture into several bowls (the number of different colors you wish to use) and add food coloring in the color you want to each separate bowl. More food coloring makes darker and brighter colors. Start with just a few drops, mix, and then add more to create the color you want.

You can combine colors to make other colors, such as red and blue for purple. For pink, add less red food coloring.

Source:
http://www.wilton.com/decorating/icing/coloring-icing.cfm

You can add decorations, as well, such as colored sprinkles, chocolate sprinkles, or even glittery sprinkles.

Source:
http://www.koyalwholesale.com

NOTE: This recipe makes $\frac{1}{2}$ cup. You may need to make multiple batches to decorate all of your cookies.

Apply icing to your cookies after they have cooled. Add sprinkles before the icing dries.

Lights for Luucy

Source:
http://www.chalicepalace.com/Chalice_Palace/Free_Stuff.html

Freezing Cookies

You might wonder why Luucy kept baking cookies with no mention of eating or distributing the cookies. That's because she FROZE her cookies until her special celebration and delivery of the various cookies that she had made!

Source:
http://www.chalicepalace.com/Chalice_Palace/Welcome.html

Baked cookies can be frozen after they have cooled completely. I know this works, my mom used to do this all the time! See section below on *To Ice/Frost or Not!*

You may wonder how to package the cookies to put in the freezer. You can put them in freezer bags and pop them into the freezer; however, the rigid containers are best, because frozen cookies can be easily broken.

Believe it or not, but you don't have to use plastic containers; you can put them in a cardboard box if you choose. With either choice, layer your cookies with a sheet of waxed paper in between the layers. This keeps the cookies from freezing together.

NOTE: If you are using a cardboard box, especially one you are recycling, line it with waxed paper or foil.

Once you have this done, put the lid on...then to make sure all the air stays out, wrap your container with plastic wrap. It makes it harder to open, but it keeps the cookies fresher.

To Ice/Frost or Not?

NOTE: In the South, people ice their cakes or cookies. In the North, people frost everything. There is a slight difference in some people's definition, ie: **Icing** is a bit thinner; **Frosting** is a bit thicker.

Source:
http://www.flickr.com/photos/57214702@N06/5627640989/

You may put the *Cookie Icing* on the cookies before you freeze them or after you take them out and thaw them.

It is more convenient to have the cookies ready to go from freezer to serving dish in many cases!

Source: Pinterest pinned from uure.com
Made from 2 caramel square candies, 1 Reese's Peanut Butter Cup, and topped with a Hershey's Kiss Flame

To freeze cookies, place them on trays in a single layer without a cover. Place in freezer. In about an hour, the frosting or icing on the cookies will be hard to the touch. Then, you are ready to package them for the freezer.

On the other hand, frosting or icing your cookies after the freezer (and totally thawed) can assure that the icing does not get chipped and all your other decorations stay intact.

Thawing Your Cookies

Thawing is probably the easiest process, because you can thaw your baked and frozen cookies on the counter or in the fridge.

Source:
http://www.chalicepalace.com

Thawing time varies, depending on packaging and volume of cookies in container. The best choice is to take them out several hours or a day in advance of when you wanted to serve them.

Source:
http://tressabelle.wordpress.com/2013/01/06/uu-chalice-cookies/

If you are in a big hurry, you can thaw them faster by one of these methods:

1. MICROWAVE: Thaw container for approximately 30 seconds and repeat if not thawed enough.
2. OVEN: Pre-heat the oven to 350°F, and bake for about 3 minutes.

NOTE: Cookies with icing may not thaw well in either Microwave or Oven, because the icing might get warm and run...then you'll have an ugly mess!!

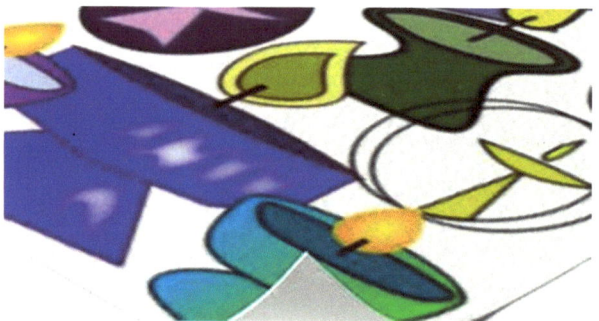

Poster available from http://www.zazzle.com

About Author

Connie Dunn
Book Coach

Connie Dunn, owner of Nature Woman Wisdom Press, Publish with Connie, and UUStoryteller, is an author, speaker and educator. Her specialty is indie publishing. She has taught writing, freelance writing, religious education, and a variety of creativity workshops.

She has been writing all her life. She has 30 years' experience as a freelance journalist working for magazines and newsletters. She won an award for her work with Small- and Home-Based Businesses with a regular column in The Dallas Morning News.

She also spent about 25 years as a Religious Educator (overlapping careers), where she wrote a *Story for All Ages* just about every week to match the minister's message.

This story came directly out of the need for teaching about all the traditions in the winter holidays from the perspective of a girl trying to make it her own Unitarian Universalist Ceremony.

Connie has a bachelor's degree in Marketing and Small Business Management. She published her first Independently Published book in 1981, which was a cookbook.

A native of Texas, she now lives in Franklin, Massachusetts, with her wife, Joyce, and their tiny Chihuahua, Rusty, and plus-size cat, Sophie.

She and Joyce are regulars at Ferry Beach, where they attend *In the Company of Women*, which is a week-long camp for women.

Other Books Written by Connie Dunn

- *A Spider, Some Thread, and a Labyrinth Walk*
- *Book Writing: Fuzzy About Where to Start?*
- *Goddess Rituals: Reclaiming Our Ancient Spiritual Heritage*
- *Miss Odell: The Privileges of Being Present for the End of Her Life - A Reality Book on Elder Care*
- *Press Releases Made Easy*
- *The Most Magical, Awesome, Delicate Creature of All*
- *The Real Story of the Dumpty Family*
- *Trees: Peaceful and Personal Meditational Poems*
- *Zoe*

For more information about these books and how to order, go to
http://www.conniedunnbooks.com/books/

To Contact Connie Dunn:
Connie Dunn, Author, Speaker, Book Coach
connie@publishwithconnie.com
http://www.publishwithconnie.com
508-446-1711

www.ingramcontent.com/pod-product-compliance
Lightning Source LLC
Chambersburg PA
CBHW042333150426
43194CB00001B/44